The Sedona GARDENS

of Saint John Vianney

Reverend J. C. Ortiz

ZITRO PRESS SEDONA, ARIZONA

planted in love —

rooted in faith

International Standard Book Number 978-0-9789750-0-5

Library of Congress Control Number 2006936741

ZITRO PUBLISHING

SAINT JOHN VIANNEY CATHOLIC CHURCH

180 Soldiers Pass Road

Sedona, Arizona 86336

928.282.7545

Printed in Canada

PRINCIPAL PHOTOGRAPHY:

Al Brown, Dave Singer, Michelle Dante

DESIGN AND PRODUCTION:

Carol Haralson

This book is dedicated to all those
who labor in the gardens of the Lord
and teach others to love.

Then he said to his disciples,
"The harvest is abundant but the laborers are
few; so ask the master of the harvest to send out
laborers for his harvest." MATTHEW 9:37-38

ACKNOWLEDGMENTS

First, my thanks to the family of faith of Saint John Vianney —
whose love has sustained me and kept me a priest.

Many who are integral to the unwritten story behind the making of a book remain unnamed by the accident of memory. Such unsung individuals form the backbone of this work. They are like the unseen skeleton that supports the body. Those who are called by name will know their spouses and partners are equally embraced. The two can never be separated. The two indeed become one entity.

I am grateful to and thank Bishop Thomas J. O'Brien, Reverend Damian Schmelz, O.S.B., Reverend Gerald Coleman, S.S., Reverends David Pettingill, Charles Kieffer and John Shetler, Greg and Karla Biddle, Jim and Joann Biddle, Thomas and Mary Bowker, Pete and Mary Fredlake, Sid E. Foutz, Daniel and Patricia Garland, Clyde and Elyse Holland, Bob and Pat Jay, James and Valerie Magar, Gordon and Helen Paravano, Ronald and Dolores Puchi, Adelfo Silva, Nancy R. Silver, David and Yvonne Singer, and David and Carol Watters.

I have one incredible parish staff. These dedicated co-workers in the vineyard support and encourage my every wild idea, and it was their generosity that allowed my attempt at this endeavor. More importantly, they are my friends. I thank for their support Robert and Teri Bays, Bruce and Sara Bissen, Jack and Sue Cleland, Brian and Kathryn Dante, Don and Irene Henkiel, Karen Kiefer, David and Rachel Lombardi, Ron and Linda Martinez, Catherine McCulloch, Elizabeth McGinnis, Ralph and Lois Pepino, Charles and Nancy Reaume, Jose and Martina Saucedo, Gil and Marcia Seevers, and Chris Warren.

A well deserved and special thanks goes as well to my "coaches" and the team who pushed this work to completion: To Carol Haralson—it took courage to take on this project. To Barbara Litrell, editor and remarkable woman of organization! And even more importantly a woman of vision. She kept me on track. To Joe Scully, co-editor and one who can spell! To Al Brown and David Singer, who are two of the best photographers in Sedona, and also mind readers. To Michelle Dante, who added the vision of youth to the illustrations, and to Bryan Rizzuto, who literally lent her a hand.

To the special cheerleaders, Dolores Puchi (also known as "Commander in Chief") and Lois Pepino, with her incredible positive energy. To Germaine and Michael Proulx, who know that the best way to calm my anxieties is to feed me. To Elizabeth Huhn—the beautiful dandelion in my garden. To Malachy and Noreen Wienges, whose kind and loving expertise was needed. To Elizabeth McGinnis. Never was there a more quiet yet staunch supporter. And to Rachel Lombardi, who types as fast as I speak! (A special thank you to Rachel's husband, David, who lent her to me from time to time.)

And to my Dad and the family who first planted and rooted. . .

Any imperfections in these memoirs and meditations are mine — although part and parcel of gardening.

As you can see, it takes a family to raise a garden — and a book.
— Fr. J.C.

In the beginning was the Word, and the Word was with God, and the Word was God. He was in the beginning with God. All things came to be through Him, and without Him nothing came to be. What came to be through Him was life, and this life was the light of the human race; the light shines in the darkness, and the darkness has not overcome it.   JOHN 1:1-5

Having just returned home from an Italian vacation, I was attempting to clear what seemed like thousands of emails from my overflowing in box when I found among them a very interesting message: The gardens of Saint John Vianney had been nominated for a beautiful public space award from the Keep Sedona Beautiful organization.

Our gardens nominated? The cultivated area directly surrounding the church and office buildings is only a small part of the fifteen-acre property. The majority of the land is raked by ravines and full of native vegetation. The garden was in reality just one of my attempts at a strategy, or more correctly a therapy, for staying sane.

When I was first ordained a Roman Catholic priest on June 1 of 1991, Bishop Thomas J. O'Brien responded to my concerns about the difficulties of celibacy, loneliness, and being family-less by suggesting I channel my energies in positive directions. One of my many interests and loves had always been plants.

I have fond memories of my grandparents and my own parents placing cuttings in damp soil, scattering seeds, and trying to grow slips of twigs and grasses given by neighbors or friends. I remember relatives transplanting faded potted plants into outdoor flower beds to revive them. One year, my siblings and cousins and I gathered the Christmas trees lined up in the alleys of our town and planted them in my family's backyard. My friend Nancy always let me plant and redo her garden on my breaks and vacations during seminary. It seems my entire life at various times included the growing and nurturing of plants.

So, following the bishop's directive, I proceeded full steam to channel this energy into making gardens of some sort or another. When I left my first parish, Saint Theresa's in Phoenix, to come to Sedona, Fr. Charles Kieffer remarked, "J. C. didn't leave a lot of space empty in our backyard." After arriving at Saint John Vianney in Sedona that last week in June of 1995, my growing compulsion continued. Early on I teasingly remarked to Greg, whose family owned the nursery at the end of the road to the church (fortunately close!), that I wanted a forest instead of dirt hills for the parish. It began slowly at first. Little by little, rocks were collected from the acreage and dry-stacked retaining walls were constructed. It seemed to occupy extra time and use all that abundant energy. More importantly, I found it created a space and time to converse with God. Plants were collected, exchanged, purchased, or revived, and the garden began to grow, along with a deeper communication with our Creator.

Throughout the years of planning and planting, a growing understanding of gardens in human history, especially in religious history, began to influence the work. The gardens began to become more alive. Gardens and plants are integral to our Judeo Christian tradition. It started at creation: Then God said, "Let the earth bring forth vegetation: every kind of plant that bears seed and every kind of fruit tree on earth that bears fruit with its seed in it." And so it happened: the earth brought forth every kind of plant that bears seed and every kind of fruit tree on earth that bears fruit with its seed in it. God saw how good it was. Evening came, and morning followed—the third day. (Genesis: 1:11-13)

Our destiny was forged in a garden with our ancestors Adam and Eve. The descendants of these two continued to plan and plant. Noah knew that at last all would be well only when an olive branch was delivered by a dove to the ark. The Exodus story has the Hebrews taking plants with them to the Promised Land. Jesus, in order to accomplish His Father's will, prayed in a garden called Gethsemane. Life ends for many of us in a resting place often called a garden, where foliage of one sort or another surrounds our markers and gravestones. Many of our ancestors sustained their lives and those of their loved ones by gardening. Through their active involvement in the trials of growing things, life itself continued. The cycle of nature is the cycle of life itself. We come into being, we grow, and we leave this world.

Gradually an initially subconscious idea became a secondary goal and then a primary one. Our garden needed some sort of foliage, bloom, or branch indicative of each season—this would help remind people as they came to the church that there is a rhythm to life and that this rhythm is the plan of a loving Creator. The garden would remind us that we are stewards of God's gift of creation and that by cooperating with God in this gift we become instruments of our God's life-giving creative force.

Our gardens at Saint John Vianney, and gardens in general, embody another important idea: that what we leave behind is much more than human remains or even memories. We leave behind the "gardens of our lives" to sustain future generations. Planning and planting a garden, watching it flourish under tender care—these liberate our innate desire to share of the "fruits" of the garden. These fruits are not just things of a material nature but include our aspirations for life as well.

In this way the garden symbolizes the journey of life.

The garden is also a place for reflection. We are beckoned there to ponder our own stories and the insights we have gathered from others. Our image of God becomes more focused. This loving Creator's graces are planted in our minds, sometimes consciously and often subconsciously, and they become clearer when we articulate them to one another.

On a personal level, the garden was a strong metaphor by which I found a fundamental approach to and meaning for my life as a priest. It provided a sense of continuity and a legacy for others in my life.

It seemed the liturgical cycle of the Catholic tradition mirrored the cycles of nature. Once again there was the cycle of life. The beginning again, the starting over, was illustrated by the planting of seeds, bringing hope of something yet to be. The care we gave to the plants so they could flourish mirrored the nourishment provided to us. We need this care and nourishment in order that we might flourish as well. In the end there was—and with grace will continue to be—the resulting fruit to be shared with others.

Throughout this "quasi memoir" you will find reflections influenced by the natural growing seasons. These reflections are also part and parcel of my experience of the human condition. There were times I found my "garden" ignored and in need of tending. At other times it was abundant and flourishing. During all times the "garden" was filled with God's presence, whether I was aware of this or not.

It is my hope that visitors, whether walking in the gardens or reading these inadequate reflections, can see something of themselves in the stories. Hopefully, if only for a few brief moments, they will pause and reflect on the gardens of their lives. Then with joy and gratitude they will see others on the same journey, and they will know how blessed and graced they are.

In the beginning, when God created the heavens and the earth, the earth was a formless wasteland, and darkness covered the abyss, while a mighty wind swept over the waters. GENESIS 1:1-2

It began, of course, in a land far, far away, in a different time and place . . . Are there not many books, movies, and tales that start that way? Actually, it usually does work that way with the triggering of a memory. A walk through the gardens of Saint John Vianney brings to heart a flood of memories, along with the faces of many who are part of the total sum. People entering the gardens around the church are doing more than walking into an area filled with foliage and plants; they are journeying into the lives of the people who call Saint John Vianney their family of faith. This set of reflections (or "edgy memoir") is one small part of the greater story.

However, back to the scope of this endeavor. . . . It happened once upon a time a long time ago during a hot week at the end of June, when a real character arrived to add one part to the total story, namely one Reverend J. C. Ortiz, a newly appointed pastor to the already established Catholic family in Sedona. What caused eyebrows to rise and tongues to wag was not so much the three moving vans and the several pickup trucks and cars of friends that arrived laden with his personal possessions. It was the content of the vehicles. Pots and pots, containers and containers, vessels of every kind containing plants, seeds, shoots, cactuses, and who knew what else.

Of course, the basic plan of Saint John Vianney's outdoor environment was in place due to the work of loving parishioners who had taken charge of caring for the plants already there. There were rosemary bushes, trees, and the native shrubs that would provide such a wonderful backbone for added embellishments to come. The space was like a tree at Christmas waiting for its lights and decorations — some store bought, some handmade, some exquisite and exotic. Often the most treasured are the plain and ordinary ones passed down through the generations.

That is the basic story. What follows was inspired by those "ornaments" to the gardens of Saint John Vianney, and the blessings they have brought.

— Fr. J.C.

The Sedona GARDENS
of Saint John Vianney

You are the light of the world. A city set on a mountain cannot be hidden. Nor do they light a lamp and then put it under a bushel basket; it is set on a lamp stand, where it gives light to all in the house. Just so, your light must shine before others, that they may see your good deeds and glorify your heavenly Father. MATTHEW 5:14-16

J A N U A R Y

The Light Fantastic

We have all been told to slow down and even at times to completely stop. However, as humans, we tend to ignore the familiar and the obvious. Deep within, we know that if we would only take the time to stop and notice the small gifts of life, our journeys might be very different. To stop and notice the little aspects of being alive can truly add so much to existence. Let's take one example—the light, a very familiar component of life so often taken for granted. Various degrees and qualities of light continuously surround us, and yet how often do we truly notice the subtleties of this gift that is an innate part of our existence?

Each season has its own characteristic light, and in Sedona the differences can be quite dramatic. Seasonal change in the light nuances color and adds dimensions distinctively different from what came before. The light of this moment is unique to the moment. It becomes apparent that the light for each time of the year is appropriate to its season. The stars in the sky on a cold winter morning seem so much closer, brighter, and alive. These stars suspended so dazzlingly close above the garden render it a whimsical fantasy befitting Disney. The bare branches of our signature cottonwood stand out against the winter blue of predawn morning. A water sprinkler on a forgotten timer has transformed its lower branches into an enchanted ice castle filled with glassy mirrors. A fantasy is created by the play of light.

Our culture attempted to slow down a few weeks back and did its best to proclaim the season of light. Although that frame of time is recently behind us, the play of light created memories that stay with us. The darkest time of the season and the shortest days of the year—winter—were met with imitation stars. Lights were hung on buildings, fences, walls, homes, trees, and shrubs and almost any structure that could hold them. This decorating for the season is perhaps a human attempt to proclaim victory of light over dark.

However, the true proclamation of light's victory is the genuine light of the season provided by God. A cold, stark, bare, simple radiance surrounds one who stops but for a few moments, allowing the chill to refocus the mind. It provides an opportunity to concentrate on the gift we have been given. The gift of the light, most importantly The Light of the World, has become one with us. The obvious quite often is ignored.

This light that has become one with us calls us to *be* light. We can be light to others and to ourselves. We stop, look at the light around us, and gain the courage to be "the gift." We are encompassed and surrounded by this light, and the world is bright!

Bare-root Roses

Look at the birds in the sky; they do not sow or reap, they gather nothing into barns, yet your heavenly Father feeds them. Are not you more important than they? Can any of you by worrying add a single moment to your life span? Why are you anxious about clothes? Learn from the way the wild flowers grow.

MATTHEW 6:26-28

One of the moving vans that accompanied me to Sedona that first summer held a collection of potted roses, rose trees, miniature roses, and even a container of wild rosebushes.

Bishop Thomas J. O'Brien once remarked that a new pastor is often much like the first son in the parable of the two sons we encounter in Matthew's gospel: A man had two sons. He came to the first and said, "Son, go out and work in the vineyard today." He said in reply, "I will not, but afterwards he changed his mind and went." (Matthew 21:28-29).

This new pastor to Saint John Vianney might complain, grumble, moan and groan, but usually in the end he managed to get accomplished what needed to be done. Then a rose collection and a wrong perception set the stage for the following twelve years. In a great "pity party" this priest was in the throes of celebrating (and it happened to be one great self-indulgent commiseration filled with sadness!) he failed to see the many other gifts and tributes of love he had received that particular Christmas season. Instead he concentrated on the only person he thought had failed to remember him (Sound familiar? How human we all can be).

As a society, we have managed to transform a season of hope, joy, and love into what can be a very melancholy time of year beset by frenetic activity. False expectations of what Christmas time should look like changes real presence into extravagant presents. This element that has encroached onto the season of love can bring disappointments, loneliness, and a downright feeling of sadness. Exchanges based on grandiose materialism and competition show their dark side when time and energy expended to produce a calculated result do not reward us with an expected or reciprocal gesture.

Finally it appeared the season was over. Life focused once again on the many daily duties of priesthood. "Fr. Pity Party" came to the resolution that following Jesus never entailed being promised a rose garden. He continued to bore many others, however, with outspoken sentiment over his disappointment. Then in mid-January came a surprise package.

Actually, it was several packages stacked outside his office door. These boxes contained the collection of bare-root rosebushes that today have found their way to various locations around the gardens of Saint John Vianney. The card that accompanied them read, "No, you were never promised a rose garden, but hopefully this will help. All my love."

Oh my! "Fr. Woe Is Me" had really never been forgotten. Fr.'s Christmas gift entailed trust on his part and waiting for the correct time to plant bare-root roses. A time that in Arizona comes about one month after Christmas.

The truth is that none of us is ever forgotten by our loving God. We just need to begin to recognize that. It is never in our own time, in our own way, in the way we think it should be according to our expectations. It is always in God's time, in God's way, and through those instruments of the Creator that we find ourselves surrounded by, usually family and friends. This is how we can experience love. We are never really forgotten, but only given ways to practice patience, increase our trust, and have faith that God continues to be in charge. After all, God sent to the world a great gift—His Son—a Real Presence.

Then he summoned his twelve disciples and gave them authority over unclean spirits to drive them out and to cure every disease and illness. MATTHEW 10:1

FEBRUARY

Healing Herbs

A bazillion years ago at Saint Patrick's Seminary in Menlo Park in northern California, I was introduced to the Ellis Peters mysteries, about a medieval English monk named Brother Cadfael. The particular detail about the monk that stuck in my mind was his herb garden. The brother's herbarium was famous. Cadfael found a great deal of tranquility among the herbs. Using his plants, he could be an amateur doctor, a Christian yenta, or even a mortician.

So, perhaps I needed a few potted herbs. These plants might calm some nerves in times that were anything but tranquil. If a few sprigs might work miracles, then a whole windowbox or two might work even better! From this grew the herb garden. Now, every year, usually in mid to late February, I take note of which herbs in the old oak barrels survived the harsh winter nights. The days will be growing longer soon, and, except for that last surprise snow (usually around Easter), it's the perfect time to take inventory and plant what is needed.

Memories come, of course. Yes, I remember Nana sending us to her garden to pick *hierba buena* for upset stomachs. It usually worked. It worked for small juvenile stomachs upset by overeating at those huge family dinners every Sunday at her house following Mass. It worked for a nervous adolescent stomach that came before asking the high school cheerleader out. It worked in calming young adult nerves when life-changing decisions had to be made. It worked when changing the course of life's journey and investigating something called seminary. Of course there were things in her backyard for earaches and toothaches, cuts, and bruises, too. There were things for burns and insect bites. Come to think of it, there was some kind of remedy for everything — even broken hearts.

Now with the memories flooding past, Fr. Damien, my first spiritual director in seminary, comes to mind. During those first two years when I was stuck in the cornfields of Indiana at Saint Meinrad, this man had the task of giving spiritual direction to a very homesick lad. Fr. Damien also had charge of a glass arboretum. This spiritual director/modern monk knew about plants. He had a south-facing glassed biology lab a couple of floors below my room. The glass roof to his botanical realm jetted out from the sandstone walls of our building. Sitting on a bedroom windowsill and looking down through the roof of the conservatory, a lonely boy from Arizona could see the displaced bougainvillea rambling all over the walls with its red bracts, and his stomach would calm.

It is a given, then. Everyone, especially pastors, must have an herb garden for healing. All the baptized are called to be healing instruments. Therefore, Saint John Vianney has herbs. Not just one type of mint, but chocolate mint, spearmint, lemon mint, peppermint, and a host of others.

(Gordon usually trims the mint in May, just in time for the Kentucky Derby—hmmm?). Pineapple sage, basil, chives, dill, oregano, cilantro, thyme, aloes, marigolds, and cayenne all mix together in the old oak barrels lining the way to the back door. The herbs grow as well under bushes, beneath this vine or at the base of this or that tree.

Often some timid mother asks for a favor in her native Spanish. Not understanding exactly what is expected, the pastor nods and follows her out to watch the cutting of some specific plants. As he waves goodbye, she rushes off with her leafy bundle to soothe some ache at home. She understands, just as those monks have throughout the ages, that we can be healing for others.

Perhaps it is not the actual concoction but the concern one has for another that heals. God is often present with us through another person in our aches and pains, in our spells of loneliness, when our hearts are broken, helping us to understand that we can be healed. We have been healed and continue to be healed, and, much more importantly, we ourselves can be healing for others. A unique poultice of concern, care, thoughtfulness, and empathy, with a large dose of love, sure can help.

FEBRUARY

Floral Messengers

Do not take gold or silver or copper for your belts; no sack for the journey, or a second tunic, or sandals, or walking stick. MATTHEW 10:9-10

There were some irises scattered here and there on the grounds of Saint John Vianney twelve years ago when I arrived. Each year I made a mental note of the colors of their blooms as they appeared in various locations at different times. Dolores says some old-time parishioners, John and Josephine, had a hand in those preliminary plantings. Also Earl—I like to call him Ike—who brings buckets of tubers to the church every time he thins his own irises. The irises are prolific. Deer seem not to want to eat them. Javelinas leave them alone. The creatures that most enjoy them and that make off with their blossoms are the two-legged ones who walk upright.

The irises, however, do indeed need to be thinned often. They should be thinned almost every year. This task has proved fortunate, as it has allowed the majority of the surrounding knolls to come alive with foliage and color. The irises, true to their folk history, are messengers. The purple ones, pale purple with a bluish tint, tend to bloom in the weeks preceding Christmas, adding the perfect Advent liturgical color to the church grounds. Their color, which is like the color of the predawn sky or the tinted rocks at evening, is echoed in the altar linens in the sanctuary. When we arrive at the church for liturgy, these flowers gently remind us to slow down.

Those deep dark purple ones, however, mostly bloom during Lent. Their majestic tint reminds us of the cloak placed on Christ before the crucifixion in Mark's gospel. I personally find it amazing, mysterious, and

yet providential all at the same time how God uses nature to paint with the appropriate shades of liturgical color. I believe it sends a heavenly message. The message of letting go of my regrets, anxieties, and controlling impulse, so as to try to live more in the present.

Those mental notes spoken of earlier concerning the various tints of the irises have allowed us to try to group them accordingly. The white ones are now planted in front of each of the outdoor Stations of the Cross, hiding the red rosebush planted there until the rose bursts forth with its own leaves and blossoms. The deep purple ones surround the perimeter of the dry-stacked rock retaining walls.

Of course, our Creator continues to remind us that God is ultimately in charge. What appear to be hybrids pop up in the midst of the predominantly white, purple, or blue blooms. These surprise "pop-ups" are white with lavender edges, and some even have streaks. We are always trying to replant and regroup, although we never seem to finish. Yep, God has other ideas. God has a sense of humor. God reminds us who ultimately is in charge.

In special spots one can find several irises with unique colors. I believe these represent specific but unknown loved ones. There is one with a very distinctive color planted by Liz for Tom. Sid dug up some from the front of his house down in the Valley that now live in front of the VIIth and VIIIth outdoor Stations of the Cross. The seventh station, one recalls, is "Jesus falls the second time." The eighth station is "Jesus speaks to the women of Jerusalem." I don't know what others feel or think when they see these particular irises blooming. The message I receive is that even our Lord fell at times, and yet got up to continue the journey. At the same time the Lord was continuing His Via Dolorosa, He managed to reach out to members of society who were marginalized, down-and-out, and treated less-than. This indeed is some message! Maybe we might let go of ourselves, put aside our own hurts and pains, and reach out in a better way to others who have an even harder row to hoe?

There is a most beautiful almost-peach-colored iris by the "thank you stone" that recognizes Bowker for all he did in his time for our parish family. I don't know where it came from, though I possibly might have an idea. This is just another secret of the gardens.

Whether we prepare ourselves and wait for the end times as we are called to in Advent, or attempt to strip ourselves of the unimportant as the Lenten season asks, or just remember those who showed us how to give, certain flowers at certain times of the year continue to serve as messengers. They remind us to be thankful for the opportunities to go beyond ourselves. They call us to be better than we are. They remind us to know God is in charge and will take care of it all. We surrender our own need for control to God's providential love. We let go of our need to call the shots and let the Creator guide us to the secrets and surprises that await us if we but embrace life with open hearts and minds.

As a body is one though it has many parts, and all the

parts of the body, though many, are one body, so also

Christ. . . . But God has so constructed the body as to

give greater honor to a part that is without it, so that

there may be no division in the body, but that the parts

may have the same concern for one another. If [one] part

suffers, all the parts suffer with it; if one part is honored,

all the parts share its joy.   1 CORINTHIANS 12:12, 24-26

MARCH

Patch of Green

One of the things visitors remark on when they come to Sedona is the "lack of lawns out west." I wonder if they know it's called a desert for a reason?

People do seem to want what they don't have. Several years back, I was preparing the grounds for a newly-ordained retreat. This getaway is for priests who have been ordained a year or less and their mentors. I decided the rectory should have its own little patch of green. Fr.'s mentor, co-conspirator, builder, inventor, great buddy, friend, and confidante, Tom, responded, "It's easier than you think."

Tom knew that we are meant to be in community. He understood that we could each use our different gifts to get a task done. An entire Saturday was spent in rolling out Kentucky bluegrass sod on what was once a driveway to the garage. Well, of course it turned out not to be easier than you think. The gravel had to be raked up and disposed of (you will never know where it is!). A sprinkler system had to be devised, but it

could only be placed after the hard caliche dirt was removed. Mike and Germaine kept exchanging those "whatever" glances, but kept rolling out the pieces of sod. The pastor truly thought they could play bocce ball and croquet (as if he or anyone coming to the retreat knew how!) on the following Monday.

The lawn went in, however, and the new priests and their mentors actually ate burgers and picnicked on a lawn that they thought had been there forever. They even tried to play croquet. The "Admiral" Dolores

provided a push mower after she caught "Fr. Bowling Green" cutting the lawn with the secretary's third pair of new scissors. What the pastor really wanted was a riding lawn mower, but it would have been bigger than the patch of lawn.

That little patch of green does, however, provide a little cool respite for bare feet on hot summer days. Whenever the grass is under his bare feet, the pastor remembers to be grateful for the people God has put in his life. The collection of golden retrievers who have lived in the rectory over the years and shared life with Fr. J. C. have also enjoyed this piece of green. Joshua, Jacobe, and now Jonaah and Jewly the cat have all napped on the grass in the shade. The pastor may also have taken a siesta or two on the grass, in thanksgiving for God's gift of friends.

What is certain is that anyone who has seen this little patch of park is reminded that it only takes love, hard work, and a team of believers to accomplish most anything. Using our God-given gifts and talents to help

others make their ideas and dreams a reality is the call of the baptized. We are reminded to be thankful for those placed in our lives who indeed make things easier. Then we are strengthened in return, to make the lives of others not only easier but also better.

Instead of thwarting the aspirations of others with jealousy and envy or with pride and ego, we can help in building the dreams of others. If you don't believe this, then take off your shoes and walk on a patch of grass that was once a gravel driveway.

Daffodils

Behold, I tell you a mystery. We shall not all fall asleep, but we will all be changed, in an instant, in the blink of an eye, at the last trumpet. For the trumpet will sound, the dead will be raised incorruptible, and we shall be changed. I CORINTHIANS 15:51-52

One of the beautiful aspects, among the many hundreds, of our Roman Catholic tradition is the fact that we involve as many of the human senses as possible in celebrating God's graces to us. Sight, smell, touch, taste, hearing — all are incorporated to help remind us that our God, our Lord Jesus, and the gift of the Spirit, grace and bless us in a very real manner continually. We focus on the grace that is ours through the new life/resurrection that is just around the corner for each of us. Pastors are frequently attempting to think of new ways in which this beauty of our tradition can be made more concrete and become more alive and apparent.

One year, in preparation for the celebration of the Feast of All Saints Day and All Souls Day, the members of our family of faith were asked to bring in daffodil bulbs in honor of our loved ones who are no longer with us. For those who may be unfamiliar with these bulbs, they are dry and brown, and their outer coverings peel off in paper-like layers. They look dead and lifeless. Baskets in front of the altar received various types of daffodil and narcissus bulbs, and even a few tulip bulbs. Our parish community is always extremely responsive and always so very good at participating in the projects and activities of the church.

The bulbs were planted on the small hills at the east side of the church about a week after their collection. Once they were in the ground, following the All Souls Day liturgies, they were forgotten. This is something we tend to do. We are always well-meaning, but so often another activity captures our attention. Plans for Thanksgiving and the upcoming holidays soon took precedent. Attention was focused on the preparation for Advent and Christmas. In the spring, as usual towards the middle of Lent, we began to tire of self-sacrifice, prayer, and almsgiving. We reverted to being very human, very busy, self-concerned. We once again began forgetting others and eased back into the patterns of our lives.

Then, just when our backs were turned, green shoots broke forth from the ground.

The javelina regards the bulbs of the tulips as a delicacy and devoured them as soon as they sprouted. But a few short weeks later there were bunches of different types of daffodils everywhere. There were the plain large King Alfred type, the double yellow, the white ones, and every combination in between. Every year now they give color to the hills, but, more importantly, they remind us that new life is truly ours. This new life is right around the corner.

These flowers call to mind that death is only part of life and the doorway to eternal life. They show us that something new, wonderful, and beautiful awaits us following what appears to be a lifeless state. The great love of God has made possible the promise of salvation. This love has made possible the reality of a new life that has no end because the Creator's Son followed the will of His Father.

The gold and white blossoms at the entrance to our spiritual home herald our upcoming celebration of the resurrection and our incorporation into it here on earth. We are reminded not to give up. We recall that our efforts of self-sacrifice, prayer, and almsgiving are not in vain. Time taken for reaching out to others is never time misspent, in spite of all the other activity we find ourselves involved in. We know that the beauty of the daffodil blooms pales in comparison to the beauty of our own resurrections that await us, if we but stay true to our baptismal call to be a people of the resurrection.

I am the true vine, and my Father is the vine grower. He takes away every branch in me that does not bear fruit, and everyone that does he prunes so that it bears more fruit. You are already pruned because of the word that I spoke to you. Remain in me, as I remain in you. Just as a branch cannot bear fruit on its own unless it remains on the vine, so neither can you unless you remain in me. I am the vine, you are the branches. Whoever remains in me and I in him will bear much fruit, because without me you can do nothing. JOHN 15:1-5

APRIL

Roses, Roses, Roses

Those who walk the grounds of the church encounter rosebushes tucked here and there, around this corner, behind that bend, in front of a statue, everywhere one would least expect. They help to give confidence, a spirit of hope, and a sense of excitement, these surprises that round the many corners of the property.

Not all our roses came from cuttings propagated from that famous original rose collection. Some of them have been gifts from parishioners, cuttings from members of our family of faith's own collections, and a

few just bought because they caught someone's eye. Each one of them is indeed a wonder. The deer seem to leave the roses alone for the most part except in a lean year. During a period of drought, when there is no food in our high desert, the new tips of the bushes are completely nipped off. This is natural pruning, so to say. In the fat times the roses are gorgeous. The different types and colors never fail to amaze not only our visitors but the locals as well. They bloom at different times for different durations and so it is possible to find the treat of a blossom or two anytime between April and December. This is a visual surprise for all of us.

Climbing rosebushes surround the statue of Our Lady of Lourdes at the east entrance of the grounds. This shrine was transported from the original church structure on Highway 89A to the present location.

The area in front of the shrine is planted in a palette of mostly pale and pastel colors as a tribute to Our Lady. Two parishioners, Clyde and Elyse, donated "Our Lady of Guadalupe" rosebushes that greet parishioners as they come through the Millennium Gates. The rosebushes by the statute of Quo Vadis were donations from the parish family in memory of two of our young men who lost their lives in a tragic car accident.

The wild roses on the east side came from cuttings found in the forest between Prescott and Jerome. These cuttings were obtained on several hikes. The rewarding delight of finding something so beautiful in such rugged terrain is yet another surprise treat from our God. It reminds me of Our Lady of Guadalupe, the Patroness of the Diocese of Phoenix, and how she surprised San Juan Diego one December long ago. She appeared before him on a rocky hill called Tepeyac in a glorious blaze of blooming roses, where surely no rose could grow.

Those rambling rosebush canes that one finds on the southeast side of the church are the remnants of the famous container rose garden that came to Sedona. They are the strong and hearty rootstock of the tree roses that did not adapt that first summer and winter in what they found to be a very different and difficult climate. They are, however, reminders that everything and everyone is salvageable. Most times, all that is needed is an opportunity, a new beginning, or a fresh start. They are comparable to that rare delight one encounters when discovering God at work in the life of someone who has opened his or her heart to His surprises. We breathe audible sighs of wonder. Rooted in Christ, we see that astonishing delights await us around every corner, even in the rockiest of soils.

APRIL

Cycle of Life

There is an appointed time for everything, and a time for every affair under the heavens. A time to be born, and a time to die; a time to plant, and a time to uproot the plant. A time to kill, and a time to heal; a time to tear down, and a time to build. A time to weep, and a time to laugh; a time to mourn, and a time to dance. A time to scatter stones, and a time to gather them; a time to embrace, and a time to be far from embraces. A time to seek, and a time to lose; a time to keep, and a time to cast away. A time to rend, and a time to sew; a time to be silent, and a time to speak. A time to love, and a time to hate; a time of war, and a time of peace. ECCLESIASTES 3:1-8

On this lazy spring Friday afternoon, Dolores and I sit on the benches in the South Gathering Area. We sit in silence now. We marveled with one another at the brilliant colors of the flowers only moments earlier. The roses are at their peak. Covered with blossoms, not one rosebush lacks a cloak of color.

The colors are almost iridescent the way the light catches the petals. We continue to sit in silence and stare, now each of us with our own individual thoughts. The California poppies at the base of the rosebushes are beyond spectacular, though they will be long gone before Mother's Day. Oh well, something is always blooming. It is not hard to find new, vibrant, and fresh flowers at this time of year.

I think, as a faded iris catches my mind, that there is something symbolic here. I continue to notice some spent and faded blooms in the background. It comes to me that this is symbolic of the parish family.

Many faces of the parish come to mind. Various people I begin to see in the flowers… Baptisms were plentiful this year! New, fresh faces staring up as water was poured over them (and only one cries!). The babies must think it is bath time. One even laughs. Our young parents are at the beginning stage of family life. The older faces of the family of faith appear as well in the background of this visual thought. These are the faces of the men and women who have moved quickly through life and are fast approaching the ultimate change. One woman last weekend, her unsteady steps guided by her loving husband, seemed somewhat lost and unsure of her whereabouts. Our Roman Catholic traditions and practices that have been so much a part of her entire life seemed vanished. There was no recognition in her eyes of who stood in vestments before her as the Body of Christ was placed in her hands. Yet, for almost twelve years previous, there had been a heartfelt smile. The dementia is firmly in place and strongly in charge. Just last week we sent another woman home, celebrating her entry into everlasting life.

It seems that more and more of the strong and wise backbones of the parish are asking for the Anointing of the Sick. They are looking for strength and grace to face the challenges that come with age. The smiles, so vibrant and fresh, that greet me before, during, and after liturgies do fade. As quickly as the flowers, we change. Our more "experienced" members fade into everlasting glory, to be replaced by newer members taking up the call to continue our family of faith. And so the cycle continues. Life is like the garden that has captured our attention. It is a mixture of the new and the faded, all planted together, each bloom providing color in its own time, adding beauty where and when it is needed.

Then I saw a new heaven and a new earth. The former heaven and the former earth had passed away, and the sea was no more. I also saw the holy city, a new Jerusalem, coming down out of heaven from God, prepared as a bride adorned for her husband. I heard a loud voice from the throne saying, "Behold, God's dwelling is with the human race. He will dwell with them and they will be his people and God himself will always be with them [as their God]. He will wipe every tear from their eyes, and there shall be no more death or mourning, wailing or pain, [for] the old order has passed away." REVELATION 21:1-4

MAY

Living Trumpets

It's just another wonderful day in Sedona (as almost every day is!). The Easter weekend celebrations are over and feel long past. Easter was early this year. The blossoms of the Easter lilies that surrounded our altar have faded. Those white blossoms that trumpeted the joy of new life in our sanctuary have found their spot out in the garden among the lilies from years past. Those lilies in the garden from former celebrations are ready to bloom. This is another symbol of the promise that the cycle of life will continue until His return.

Yet, the Easter lilies planted last year in the garden call us back to the present. These blooms remind any visitors to the secret garden that we continue our celebration of resurrection. Almost everything is blooming as the last days of spring make their way into the extremely hot days of summer. However, it is these Easter lilies that are most prominent in the garden. They demand one's attention. Everything else seems to

take a back seat. The trees are that fresh new green color. In a few short weeks they will become that deep green one associates with summer. For now, they hint as well toward newness. Almost everywhere one looks there is a sign—a reminder of new life, again most especially signaled by those Easter lilies.

Tonight the Saturday evening vigil liturgy has concluded. The hustle and bustle around the church has quieted. It leaves an opportunity to walk the church grounds and be reminded of God's great lessons, and, more importantly, moved to thankfulness for them. These blessings are countless. How do we let ourselves continually forget that we are showered with His love? Perhaps it is the out-of-control activity of our modern existence that keeps us from stopping to spend even a few moments in gratitude.

It promises to be a warm and balmy spring evening once the sun finally decides to set. This is another gift given to us. These evenings are still filled with enough light to enjoy our surroundings before darkness comes. On this particular evening I find almost an extra hour has been provided. This is time to reflect. This is an opportunity to be mindful of a loving Creator and to spend time thanking God for the people who have become my family here in the Red Rocks. The words from this evening's gathering song continue to echo in the mind. These lyrics are indeed indicative of why we are moved to do great things. "This is the feast of victory for our God, Alleluia, alleluia, alleluia. . . " We are indeed a victorious people, because that Easter resurrection has been won for us. The grounds of the parish echo this sentiment all around the church building. That very distinct "spring green" color once again catches the imagination and points toward newness. That special color almost only found this time of year symbolizes something new and fresh. The flowers and shrubs with their blossoms remind us that we too will bloom. Once again it is the Easter lilies though, that most poignantly trumpet the new life that surrounds us.

We too have the ability to start again. We too try yet one more time to be a new entity. It's great to be a member of His resurrection people. It is wonderful to be a living trumpet of life eternal. "This is the feast of victory for our God."

Rain!

I will sprinkle clean water upon you to cleanse you from all your

impurities, and from all your idols I will cleanse you. I will give you

a new heart and place a new spirit within you, taking from your

bodies your stony hearts and giving you natural hearts.

EZEKIEL 36:25-26

It's raining! Actually, it's only sprinkling. However, rain is rain for Arizonans. We so need this wonderful gift, especially in this year of drought! We are halfway through the month and the promise of rain brings a reminder of hope. Here in Sedona, the day can start off with a bright sunny morning. In a couple of hours fluffy puffs of white cloud begin to float by. Then gray clouds. Pretty soon the darker clouds hide the sunshine. Thunder rumbles in the distance, and tiny drops begin to fall. We are very desperately in need of this gift.

So often one forgets we live in a desert, albeit a high desert. Therefore water is at a premium and a treasured gift. The Native Americans chose Oak Creek Canyon in which to live, where there was a running source of this precious commodity. Hundreds of years later it remains for us who live in this area a very precious commodity.

So when the air is permeated with that familiar smell (I have yet to be able to articulate this sweet scent, for it is far more than the smell of wet dirt) and clouds are suspended in the distance, we begin to look for and expect the treasured rain. The rain brings a sense of hopefulness. A quiet joy comes over us. It will only be a short respite from the heat. It will be a recess, if only for a day, from the routine. It will be freedom from having to drag out the garden hose.

It is also an excuse to allow ourselves to get wet, to be cleansed. It brings back memories of those days of youth walking home from school in the rain not caring how wet we got.

The rain in May is usually warm and falls softly. It advertises that relief from classrooms and the work routine is right around the corner. It signals that summer vacations are close at hand. It is also an indication that the air and our environment are being cleansed naturally.

May showers signal as well that the monsoons are on their way. The monsoons are that desert phenomenon of heavy summer rains with their prelude of nature's fireworks. They bring lightning and crescendos of loud thunder to our Red Rock area. The outside ramadas, the patios, and the large windows in the church and office areas become theatres where we watch God cleanse the world. During the summer rains, the arroyos, washes, and creeks swell with water that at times is even life-threatening. Sometimes it takes an awful lot of water to get something clean! When the monsoons come, it seems as if heaven itself has opened.

For now, we will have to be content with this delicate sprinkle. The gentle nature of the rain allows us, if we wish, to be misted while venturing around the garden watching the dust depart from leaves and the rose

blossoms glisten with new moisture. It reminds us of the wonderful gift of Baptism, the spiritual cleansing of the old, and the symbolic ritual of the beginning of opportunity for the new. This gentle sprinkling calls us to choose to live out of our baptismal cleansing. Catching sight of a full half arc of rainbow, another symbol of God's covenant to humanity, one cannot help but be moved. We remember that we too are called to assist in protecting God's promise of full lives for all. This is another part of the Christian baptismal call. Cleansed, we help others to embrace the ability to be washed clean and start anew.

To anyone who has, more will be given and he will grow rich; for anyone who has not, even what he has will be taken away. This is why I speak to them in parables, because they look but do not see and hear but do not listen or understand. MATTHEW 13:12

JUNE

Pink and Gold

It must be June! The majestic color of the yellow-gold coreopsis adds brightness to the area fronting the outdoor Stations of the Cross. Mixed almost equally among the gold is a soft, calming pale pink hue. This color is provided by the evening primrose. Both varieties of plants began as clumps the size of a clenched fist. The pink primroses were given by dear friends, Dan and Trish, one year when they renewed their garden for the season. The church became the recipient of their gift, these pink flowers. The gold came from a pot brought from Phoenix in one of those infamous moving vans.

The hills are now covered each May in both colors. The old and the familiar mix with the new and the exciting. Both growing together just as in human life. One might expect the old and familiar to have a soft and reassuring color. As well, the new and exciting might be expected to come in a bold hue. But, as with most of the preconceived notions we hold, some element challenges our expectation, helping to change and broaden

our views on life. The known gives courage to embrace the uncertain. The new provides an invigorating sentiment that lures us forward. Both colors provide an impetus to take on this gift called life.

When the parish family notices the bright gold and the pink, an inevitable mist of undeniable love envelops each one's very being. We gain courage to continue living the gospel message. Here is another metaphor we find blooming in our gardens.

Day after day, opportunities are provided to move us out of our comfortable ruts. We often don't understand where we are being called to move toward, but our faith guides us there. We are asked to move into light and love. We have known soft caressing love. We usually expect it to be signified by those pale pink flowers. The truth is that sometimes the soft caressing love promises something new and exciting. The bright gold reminds us of the brightness of the past accomplishments. The old and familiar triumphs grant us courage. The gold is a call to try again because we have known success. It is a familiar and reassuring feeling. The pink spurs us on to new endeavors because we have been loved. The pink and gold are entwined in a dance of reversals.

Most would expect the gold to signify the new and the pink the familiar. In this case, the unknown, the new that brings something exciting, came in a form perceived as pale and soft. With the pink primrose came a new friendship. The old and the familiar takes the form of a flower that is so bright in color, the golden coreopsis. This was provided to me through an old and endearing friendship. Life is full of the unforeseen and the unexpected. Life contains so many elements wonderfully juxtaposed. Life is full of irony. Looking at the faces of those in the pews and thinking of their stories confirms this. A deep sentiment begins to flower. One just never knows.

Rare Days

See what love the Father has bestowed on us that we may be called the children of God. Yet so we are. The reason the world does not know us is that it did not know him. Beloved, we are God's children now; what we shall be has not yet been revealed. We do know that when it is revealed we shall be like him, for we shall see him as he is. Everyone who has this hope based on him makes himself pure, as he is pure. 1 JOHN 3:1-3

I love June. It reminds me of the famous lines from that poem by James Russell Lowell: "And what is so rare as a day in June? Then, if ever, come perfect days; Then Heaven tries earth if it be in tune, And over it softly her warm ear lays." The days do indeed seem perfect. It is hot, but the heat is not unbearable yet. The change in routine and the change in season is still novel. The ability to sleep in is still fresh and has not become tired with the tedious and usual activity. We haven't reached the point where we remain in bed out of boredom with a common

routine. The months preceding June were filled with the need to get up earlier for classes, jobs, or athletic endeavors. Now the opportunity to sleep in is yet maiden and refreshing.

The mornings are cool enough to sit out on the patio and enjoy coffee and a roll or pastry. The afternoons are warm enough to swim or play in the creek without too much chill. The evenings are pleasant. These evenings are so pleasant that one wants to sit outside and enjoy the atmosphere of newness and cleanliness. The evenings are clear and

the stars are out. Sometimes the sun sets just as the moon is rising, and both are visible. We question whether one day we can indeed have it all. It is truly almost perfect. The garden is fully leafed out. The plants are still giving color. The blossoms and the vegetables are beginning to ripen. Tomatoes are turning that unique pink before they become deep red. Other vegetables have only to gain size, for their final shape is already evident. That fresh newness of everything seems to surround us.

Everything seems so new and full of hope. It allows one to feel joy in the now while still longing for the yet-to-come. This is reminiscent of our lives as Christians. Of course we still live in the present. Yet we look forward to that which is to come. It is a treat to walk barefoot on the cool grass and feel it tickle. It is a joy to see the blue spruces with their new buds and know something wonderful is coming. There is anticipation of watermelons and sweet corn so close to ripeness that your mouth begins to water and yearn for them. The geraniums are one mass of red color in their pots. The itty-bitty green lemons pose the promise of full-grown yellow fruit that will be cut and immersed in iced tea. The figs still small

THE KISS OF THE SUN FOR PARDON
THE SONG OF THE BIRDS FOR MIRTH
ONE IS NEARER GODS HEART
IN A GARDEN
THAN ANYWHERE ELSE ON EARTH

and green pledge the treat they will be when placed on marzipan and crostini. The orange blooms of the pomegranate bush guarantee round juicy finger-staining joys one day soon as well.

I can't help but think of that scene in Cecil B. DeMille's *Ten Commandments*. It is the Exodus scene that shows the Hebrews finally set free. They enjoy the now and they long for what is yet to come. The ancestors of our Jewish brothers and sisters gather in the Avenue of the Sphinxes with their little fig trees, pomegranate bushes, date palm sprigs, and grapevine cuttings among their possessions. They plan to carry these to the land of milk and honey and live out something new. The movie narrator tells us that they are "the planters of vineyards and the sowers of seeds; each hoping to sit under his own vine and fig tree."

Here all around me are the various sprigs and shoots that helped to make something new in the high desert of Sedona. The grapevines now cover the viga and latilla arbor off the common room. The berry bushes transplanted from the banks of Oak Creek are maturing and illustrate that the promise of newness is true and alive.

As the garden greenery with its yield ripens towards full prime, we are reminded that we too wait for the full realization of what we are truly about. We are on a journey. The journey of life is to be enjoyed now with the certainty that we are being seasoned with hope to enjoy one day our true prime. The Easter promises of Jesus were celebrated a few weeks ago, and yet more newness and freshness continues to come.

The promise of our potential feels so real when surrounded by the promising potential of the garden. The plants point toward that almost inconceivable fantastic future of transfiguration that awaits the baptized. This unrealized developing possibility will come throughout our lives. Our human life is a perpetual state of journey. That is, until the reward of everlasting life is ours. Then we will enjoy the result of who we truly are. It is true nothing is more rare than days like these. Days that show the reality of the hope and promise that is ours.

Clouds and Junipers

As you know, we treated each one of you as a father treats his children, exhorting and encouraging you and insisting that you conduct yourselves as worthy of the God who calls you into his kingdom and glory. 1 THESSALONIANS 2:11-12

There are an extraordinary few days when the garden seems to call out more loudly than usual. I am drawn to seek out the old gnarled, twisted junipers on the property. I sit on the boulders that surround them or lay on the ground to place those big fluffy clouds in the sky behind them or to one side or the other. Sometimes I like to position my head so I can see the clouds through the junipers. I visually paint a scene by moving my field of vision and placing the clouds in various positions to frame the junipers.

I have wondered what brings this altered awareness of the garden, but it is still a mystery to me. I know it happens year after year. Always, it catches me by surprise. I have become aware of this unique unnamed "personal season" of mine. It happens the moment there is a sense of being "in between." It happens for me in the crook of the year, where spring bends toward summer. I should coin a unique and appropriate title for this new season, for these special days, as we have for Indian Summer. I have yet to find one that is appropriate. I have yet to find one that describes the sentiments of this season that contain, among others, an indescribable joy.

I know that when "my season" arrives, the direction of my thoughts and memories will take a familiar turn. There is a sense that one season has not completely left. Spring is lingering. The next season has not fully swept down on us. Summer still smiles from a distance. These are those rare few days when everything that surrounds me melds together. The temperature, the colors of the plants, the shades of the flowers, the smell of the earth — all blend together into one entity. This includes almost all that can be seen, tasted, or felt — everything fuses into one all-encompassing wave of love and gratitude.

I begin to have more and more thoughts of Papa Jody. That is the name we have given Dad. This is not to say that I don't think of my father at other times of the year. I do. But this incomprehensible merging of

the present with past and future, sensed through the garden, focuses my gratitude for so many influences in my life, most especially Dad. Some have attributed to Mark Twain the comment, "When I was a boy of fourteen, my father was so ignorant I could hardly stand to have the old man around. But when I got to be twenty-one, I was astonished at how much the old man had learned in seven years."

The older I get the smarter my father does become. I finally have realized my siblings and I did not come with a set of instructions. Dad really did his best. Like those old native junipers, Dad has weathered the clouds of life. Some of those clouds my brothers and sisters and I moved into his life. Some were thunderheads, and some were rolling mounds of white that the sun shot through in gold rays. All of them changed his view, as well as ours, for the better.

The added clouds sufficed to make a picturesque scene. The clouds and storms in life can help to make us who we are. Perhaps we become more gnarly, but far more interesting and more stable. I find my attention as well intently focused on that spirit of gratitude I spoke of earlier. The sentiment of being grateful seems missing from our contemporary society. There are indeed thankful people in our world. Most of us have moments when we acknowledge those people and blessings we are thankful for. There are times when we are simply grateful. We even have in this country a day at the closing of autumn set aside for the entire country to be thankful.

Yet it still feels that an all-pervasive day-to-day gratitude is hidden in our society. Sometimes we are all caught up in the activity and the emotional demands of life. This prevents us from truly being a people with a spirit of gratitude. We need Thanksgiving Day. I need a private special season. Roman Catholics need the ritual of thanksgiving — the Eucharist. All these reminders call us to invite gratitude into our lives. We are called to have a spirit of gratitude for our blessings.

I have been given a teacher. I am grateful that the "apple doesn't fall far from the tree." It has given me a chance to see the totality of life — the good and the not-so-good — as growth, and even blessing. I have been given a human example. I am grateful in a special way for the junipers and the clouds that sometimes surround them. I am most appreciative, truly thankful, for Dad.

Chastised a little, they shall be greatly blessed, because God tried them and found them worthy of himself. As gold in the furnace, he proved them, and as sacrificial offerings he took them to himself. WISDOM 3:5-6

JULY

Crepe Myrtles

O h! The crepe myrtles are in full bloom. They signal that despite the already high temperatures a real scorcher is in store for us. All over our town of Sedona and most especially all over the grounds of Saint John Vianney, the crepe myrtle bushes are bowed down with the weight of numerous fragile blossoms. The sidewalks are covered with delicate white, lavender, pink, and red blossoms that have already fallen. The overused cliché "but it's a dry heat" offers no consolation. Hope, nevertheless, is inherent in these summer blossoms, and therein lies the consolation.

Thriving in spite of the heat, and probably because of the heat, these blossoms remind us that heat can be purifying. An extreme circumstance can strengthen our faith. Natives of Arizona and others who have weathered its summers have survived this heat. We are experienced and toughened due to previous infernos.

Aunt Lucy's Fishpond

Then Jesus came from Galilee to John at the Jordan to be baptized by him. John tried to prevent him, saying, "I need to be baptized by you, and yet you are coming to me?" Jesus said to him in reply, "Allow it now, for thus it is fitting for us to fulfill all righteousness." Then he allowed him. After Jesus was baptized, he came up from the water and behold, the heavens were opened [for him], and he saw the Spirit of God descending like a dove [and] coming upon him. And a voice came from the heavens, saying, "This is my beloved son, with whom I am well pleased." MATTHEW 3:13-17

Aunt Lucy is my great aunt. In reality she is my mother's aunt. But it was easier to call her Aunt Lucy than to explain to everybody what seemed a complicated lineage when we were young. Aunt Lucy lived across the street from us and was quite a character. Come to think about it, this being a character apparently

comes quite honestly to our family. I realize now I came from a long line
of characters. It was a joy to venture across the street and listen to Aunt
Lucy pontificate on almost any subject. We thought she knew everything.
Her yard was better than Legend City, that long-gone Arizona theme
park. She had a fishpond in her backyard in the shade of what seemed
then a huge tree. As a youngster, I coveted that small body of water. The
fish and all kinds of swimming things, buzzing things, and blooming things

were captivating. And so a plan was devised. The project slowly took form in the after-school hours of that year of junior high and continued into the following summer. It entailed digging a multi-layered hole that I hoped would hold water. The hole needed an island in the middle just like my great aunt's. At the local lumberyard we found cement that could be mixed in a wheelbarrow with only water, plus lots of energy and muscle.

Writing these thoughts shows me more clearly how our experiences throughout life indeed color who we are and the character of the person we become. Our backgrounds influence the expectations we place on ourselves. They contribute to forming what we think our needs are throughout life. They help to instill what might subconsciously drive us.

One hot July day, I returned in memory to a time long ago when the need for water eventually resulted in a backyard fishpond. The Saint John Vianney garden needed a body of water like the one inspired by Aunt Lucy's pond. Our birdbaths were not large enough. They had to be filled every day, especially when temperatures were over 100° and it was so darn hot. The sound of water has been proven to bring tranquility and calm our inner emotions. So began the digging of a multi-layered hole (sans island). "Father J. C. is digging a hole." "What's he up to now?" "He is going to baptize the Catechumens outside next Easter in that hole!" Oh, it was none of that. Basically, we just needed water. We needed to see it. We needed to hear it. We needed to touch it.

There is something spiritual about water. Jesus used water in his life and ministry. Let's face it: Without water there is no life. We need water to live. Another thing we need, whether we want to admit it or not, is God. And we need physical manifestations of God's loving, embracing arms. We need each other.

Any time of year that one steps into the garden and wanders past the pond, calmness seems to come. This body of water in the backyard is an invitation. It is a call to stop, ponder, and give thanks for the gift of life and all the gifts in our lives. Most especially on hot July days when the water lilies bloom in the tinkling water above flashes of darting gold, when bees and dragonflies are buzzing, there is the innate knowledge that we continue to be sustained daily.

We are washed clean and our lives sustained not solely by water or by bread alone but by God. Most often this realization comes to us through each other. When we live out this realization and reach out to one another we can be assured that God is pleased with us.

You visit the earth and water it, make it abundantly fertile. God's stream is filled with water; with it you supply the world with grain. Thus do you prepare the earth: you drench plowed furrows, and level their ridges. With showers you keep the ground soft, blessing its young sprouts. You adorn the year with your bounty; your paths drip with fruitful rain. The untilled meadows also drip; the hills are robed with joy. The pastures are clothed with flocks, the valleys blanketed with grain; they cheer and sing for joy.   PSALM 65:10-14

AUGUST

Hot, Heavy, and Low

There is something about August that signals a slowing down. It is not the slowing down toward an end, but the slowing down of an awareness of abundance. It is far more than the fact that it has been so hot for so long and we are just tired of it. There is a physical density to the entire environment. Everything feels heavy, everything is full, and everything hangs low. The wonderful sweet corn down the highway is heavy with moisture and sweetness. The grapes hang low on the vines. What is left of the fruit hangs so low on the tree branches it almost pulls them to the ground. The sky, the air, the entire atmosphere feels engorged. Life itself feels full, and indeed it is. Here is one more time to celebrate that fullness of life, to take on a stance of gratefulness. We are so blessed, we are so gifted, and we are so loved. Blessings abound. Gifts surround us. Love is innate in who we are as a people of God. This love is overwhelming. It is almost impossible not to feel how loved into existence we are.

The words of the evangelist John come to mind: For God so loved the world that he gave his only Son, so that everyone who believes in him might not perish but might have eternal life. (John 3:16). Everywhere one looks are examples that conjure visions of grace. Everywhere one looks, the fullness of time is evident. The smell of the entire North Country, especially the Red Rock area, is ripe with bounty. The taste of the summer harvest invites us into thankfulness for the good gifts of the earth. The touch of the air reminds us of a full storehouse of blessings.

Our entire existence is swollen with God's unconditional love. It will be almost three more months before our entire nation stops for a day of thankfulness. But we are provided days now in which to practice gratitude in the present. The beginning of our awareness and the start of our gathering begin this day, in the here and now, at the end of summer.

It will be at least a month and a half until the temperature begins to cool. We have several weeks yet to take in the realization of the abundance of God's creation. We have a few more weeks to reap the gifts of the garden. We have days to enjoy what has been provided for us. We have a lifetime to be a thankful people in response to God's abundance for us. We start now in the present.

AUGUST

Into the Desert

At once the spirit drove him out into the desert, and he remained
in the desert for forty days, tempted by Satan. He was among wild
beasts, and the angels ministered to him. MARK 1:12-13

When I went away to seminary I found myself surrounded
by the cornfields of southern Indiana. It was there that
I realized how much I loved the deserts of Arizona.

Thousands of generations have passed, but perhaps there remains
still a bit of the desert wanderer in our blood. That was the first time I had
ever lived outside of Arizona for a period of time. I became grateful for
the obvious I had taken for granted.

When traveling from Phoenix to Tucson or from Phoenix to
Flagstaff, if we open ourselves to the obvious possibility, we encounter a
harsh beauty often ignored. The colors change almost minute by minute.
The Palo Verde trees range from green to blue. The ironwood trees appear

misted in a purple haze during certain times of the year. Even the lacy mesquite trees in spring are beautiful with their own blossoms.

It is the cactuses, though, that are most interesting for me. There is such a wide array of shades to the cactus. The colors of their blossoms are equally amazing. The hues range from pure white to sizzling purples and pinks. There are bright yellows as well as reds and oranges. I headed off to take cactus cuttings that first Thanksgiving break when I came home from seminary. I raided the homes of all my neighbors and friends and their neighbors and friends. I even went to "the cactus store," feeling like a tourist, to purchase some small containers of unique cactuses I was unable to find in my backyard invasions.

Terra cotta clay pots were packed in bubble wrap and newspaper and shipped off. Instead of shipping the cactuses, however, I wrapped them in paper towels and newspaper and nestled them between jeans and tee shirts in the bags I would carry on the airplane. It worked! Except for the fact that the first time I wore those jeans I itched like crazy. Back at the seminary I proudly displayed in one corner of my cell a piece of my very own desert. These poor specimens have over the years been hauled from place to place and parish to parish. Some of the pots are cracked and chipped. Many still hold their original cuttings, now grown. Some of the cactuses have been attacked by predators. Every summer throughout those seminary years, I collected cactuses. John helped me one summer to add to my little desert, and he started his own.

Greg didn't realize the happiness he created when he landscaped the ravine side of the addition to the parking lot with cactus cuttings. When people venture out to the far edge of our new parking lot, which many tourists do indeed do in order to take pictures, they find bright yellow, purple, and pink blooms. One Lent, our art and environment team graced the sanctuary with ocotillos to illustrate our journey with Christ into the desert. Of course, they were later planted on the grounds. They bloomed like bright red torches when the monsoon season arrived. One ocotillo continues to survive almost nine years later in its hidden spot protected by native brush. It gives away its hiding place every time it sends out its red flame. This happens once a year, usually in August.

When ordination to the priesthood came, I decided to decorate with cactuses for the celebration of my first Mass of Thanksgiving and the reception that followed. My classmates had thought the desert in my room a bit peculiar, one of many reasons they perceived this soon-to-be-ordained priest as a character. But the cactuses were the perfect enhancement for this special first Liturgy. One in particular was ready to bloom. On June 1, the day of ordination, it indeed offered up the most exquisite iridescent flowers directly in front of the altar. To this very day, it still blooms every year precisely on June 1. I see this as an anniversary gift. Dolores calls every year to inquire if the cactus has fulfilled its promise. It was growing so long that the tips broke off and now they are planted on the southwest side of the church under St. Francis's watchful gaze. Bob adds his agaves to the grounds every now and then. He has contributed several different varieties. They do well if the ground squirrels don't get to them before they have time to mature and become tough.

Here at Saint John Vianney we have our very own means of going into the desert. We can walk, explore, and finally find the way to our cactuses. Thank God (literally), we don't have to wander in the desert for forty days or for forty years.

Led into our own miniature representation of the desert, we can come to grips with the temptations in our own lives, ask God for strength, and leave our burdens and temptations behind.

Give and gifts will be given to you; a good measure,

packed together, shaken down, and overflowing, will be

poured into your lap. For the measure with which you

measure will in return be measured out to you.   LUKE 6:38

SEPTEMBER

The Harvest

Most people like to reserve the giving of gifts for birthdays, anniversaries, Christmas, or to mark the special events of life. There is nothing wrong with this. Any time is a good time to give and share. When I look around, I see the gift of a world and the gift of life that is so completely filled with blessings. Those blessings are abundant! There are times when, like many people, I forget this fundamental fact. Instead of seeing the abundance, the focus of my attention becomes the hole, the lack, what is missing.

The gardens, however, point to the real truth. There the real truth of plenitude is gloriously demonstrated. It only takes a short jaunt through our gardens to refocus on blessings. A short change of venue brings a total change of environment — simply by leaving the buildings. Outside one can place oneself in God's creation and clear the mind, shift the focus to the absoluteness of the reality of the truth.

We are abundantly blessed! The gardens of our parish fundamentally demonstrate this. At this particular time in the growing season—late summer—abundance is the norm. The herbs, the tomatoes, and the vegetables have been harvested nonstop for the last several months. The plants are yielding blossoms for the decoration of home, office, and church once again. It is not uncommon for an inch of rain to fall on us in one hour one day. The sun can then flood us with dazzling brilliance the very next day. All brings joy.

Instead of waiting for a special occasion to share our joys and blessings, we are moved to share everything every day. We begin to

understand that every day is a special event. Every day we have been given is a special blessing to be shared with others. This task is simply accomplished by sharing our lives with one another. It is truly as simple as combining a glass of wine, a loaf of fresh bread, and the company of a trusted friend. This combination calls for a celebration. This is blessing. This is indeed a special event. This is an inevitable, honest, and frank domestic Eucharist.

We can harvest our love for one another. We can add the gift of the gardens and an impromptu celebration takes place. A fitting feast to rival the best planned "special" event or holiday. For this is a special event. It is the realization that our blessings are overflowing. We are totally surrounded and encompassed by God's gifts. Aware of this abundance, we share with those around us as God has shared with us. We don't wait for a special season or event. Every day is special. Every day is an event.

Forest Mosaic

They are like a tree planted near streams of water, that yields its
fruit in season; Its leaves never wither; whatever they do prospers.

PSALM 1:3

I remember that first time I remarked to Greg that I wanted a forest
for the parish. Greg just looked at me in that way he does when he
sorts through one of my ideas. He had that look that gives away
his suspicion that another of the pastor's undertakings will involve a lot
more time and energy than the pastor realizes. He remained silent. But I
was told as a boy that every human being should have a dream of his or
her own, maybe more than one. I set out to make the dream of a forest on
the southeast side of the property a reality.

Greg picked out a few trees and brought out the necessary equipment
to plant them. I picked out plants as well and placed them. West Fork

in Oak Creek Canyon had lately become the choice of location for hiking and outdoor activities. The leaves were beginning to turn. They provided a beautiful picture of autumn. Therefore, "back at the ranch," red maples, birch, and aspen had to be incorporated into our forest. Oak trees as well were transplanted. The banks of Oak Creek and several locations in the canyon are covered with wild vinca. And so—you guessed it—clumps of vinca made their way to new homes under our trees. Junipers filled out the gentle slope of the sidewalk from the east entrance of the church south to the back parking lot. Here and there some pyracantha filled in the visual holes along with rock cotoneaster at their bases.

Native tree and brush volunteers sprang up here and there and were left to grow. I hate to see anything not given a chance. I dislike drastic pruning as well. John and I go round and round debating his need to see everything pruned. My idea is to allow the foliage to be free. Oh, of course I know some trimming is needed. It even says so in the parables. I feel as little trimming as possible will produce the desired goal of a forest. After all, a forest should be a bit wild, unkempt, careless, and perhaps appear disordered.

Our forest at Saint John Vianney should indeed be free. Life is not perfectly ordered, as our own lives demonstrate. Forests are like a mosaic. Step back and we see the total beautiful picture. Step close and we find the many components that are needed to compose the whole. Even in chaos, the Lord can create order and make beauty.

When something appears wild, perhaps one should only stop, discern, and search. There may be a gift waiting. There might be a gift that arises from freedom lying under a seemingly obvious cover. We encounter small surprises and gifts hidden here and there in our forest. We might even find a hidden gift in our own lives. It only takes the will to stop, look more closely, and perhaps surrender. One can surrender preconceived ideas or notions about how something, or even someone, should be or look. We might have a tendency in our own landscaping, and indeed in our lives, to think we know how the final outcome should be. We tend to do it with people as well. Outward appearances are indeed deceiving and misleading. We all know that. The entire person is composed of many elements, experiences, and situations that make them who they are. At times we take one element of the total person and attempt to define them based solely on this factor.

God is one of those components in each of our lives. We are made in the image and likeness of God. We are a totality of the experiences of our lives as well. A proposed question then: What might we learn if we surrender our own agendas and ideas about others and ourselves and leave some room for freedom? We might discover a more beautiful and total portrait.

Rejoice in the Lord always. I shall say it again: rejoice! Your kindness should be known to all. The Lord is near. Have no anxiety at all, but in everything, by prayer and petition, with thanksgiving, make your requests known to God. Then the peace of God that surpasses all understanding will guard your hearts and minds in Christ Jesus. Finally, brothers, whatever is true, whatever is honorable, whatever is just, whatever is pure, whatever is lovely, whatever is gracious, if there is any excellence and if there is anything worthy of praise, think about these things. . . PHILIPPIANS 4:4-8

OCTOBER

Bloom Where You Are Planted

Change is in the air. As I walk out onto the deck, I have the very slight perception of cooler air. I look out on the yellow leaves of the cottonwood and remember the first time I saw it — it was then a three-inch volunteer.

It was the summer of 1995 and I had just been transferred to Saint John Vianney. I was standing pretty much in this same location looking down on the rocks and dirt that surrounded the church so abundantly. There were feelings of excitement about being the new pastor, but there were also feelings of doubt and loneliness. I had just left the thousands of families, a Catholic school, and myriad activities that go along with a large parish. I basically knew no one at my new parish. Although many people had introduced themselves to me in my first two weeks, I couldn't remember if that woman walking by was Mary or Sue or Joan. I questioned my "yes" to the bishop.

As I glanced down at a seam in the sidewalk, I noticed a patch of green that didn't seem to belong there. I raced down the stairs, glad to have a diversion from unpacking. As I approached, that fragile sliver of green continued to beckon. Upon investigating a tiny three-inch shoot with a few leaves, I decided it was a cottonwood tree. Knowing how large these trees can become, I pondered moving it so it would not ruin the concrete sidewalk as it got bigger. But then I remembered one of those wall hangings with its "bumper sticker" philosophical saying. It had been a farewell gift from my last parish. I had just seen it while going through the forest of boxes. It was inscribed with Mary Engelbreit's words, "Bloom where you are planted."

At that moment, I made a silent pact with this tree that I wouldn't pull it out or cut it down as long as it would grow. The tree became a symbol of growth wedged in an environment that might be hostile, surroundings that might even appear to prevent growth. All these years later, as I look at this towering tree — now more than thirty feet tall — dressed in its xanthic cloak, I realize that with endurance, fortitude, and some patience thrown in, one can indeed bloom where one is planted.

If you look to the north while driving away from town on Highway 179, at times you can see the top of our cottonwood tree against the walls of the church. No matter what season we are in, or whether our cottonwood is appareled in bright green branches or auric leaves, or is naked in winter, it always seems to beckon a warm welcome to all.

Olives and Lemons

Indeed, the grace of our Lord has been abundant, along with the faith and love that are in Christ Jesus. 1 TIMOTHY 1:14

Pete and Mary herded a group of "Red Rockers" through Italy several years ago. Rome captured their attention acutely, but perhaps not enough notice was given to Tuscany. A night in Florence, rides through a countryside patchworked with various crops, traveling walled city to walled city—it was a whirlwind. It was curious, then, that on evenings spent reminiscing about this area, it was the countryside that returned to me most clearly. The olive groves, the vineyards, the herbs, the pots of flowers — these were what filled the mind of the daydreaming pastor.

When opportunity presented itself to attempt painting for an almost two-week stay at a villa in one of the smaller towns of this section of Italy—there was no choice. No decision to be made. Living in an old convent that had become a working farm with olive groves and vineyards

cemented both novel and seasoned ideas about how to bring a bit of Tuscany to the "secret patio" back in Sedona.

The patio between the classrooms and the rectory had a foundation of exposed red tinted aggregate and was the perfect place for pots of bright red geraniums. It was now the correct location to add a potted fig tree, a couple of pots of lemon trees, and potted lavender scattered here and there. Of course if there was lavender there had to be various types of rosemary and a pomegranate bush, herbs, and succulents. As everything tends to around Saint John Vianney, it took on a life of its own. Italy confirmed the notion of abundant pleasure (already a premise in liturgical celebrations in our parish) and the pots of plants added to the already full patio made it indeed abundant.

Although painting is great, life is art in and of itself. To walk out into this space focuses attention on the fact that we are the artists of our own lives. God has provided the canvas on which we use our gifts and talents to help in creating a masterpiece the Lord can take delight in.

Here we are surrounded by the types of plants, trees, and herbs that missionaries of Mediterranean descent carried with them as carefully

guarded twigs and shoots on their long voyage to the desert Southwest. Here we feel continuity with the past and a sigh of contentment that the legacy will continue. It is much like the legacy that continues with our Roman Catholic traditions and the Word of God we continue to pass on to newer generations.

It won't take much next summer, this fantasy paints, to walk out, pick some tomatoes and basil from the old oak barrels, heap them on some sliced mozzarella, and drizzle it all with olive oil carried home from Italy between socks and underwear. It will be a perfect time to take advantage of the opportunity to offer visitors some of our abundance. It will be a perfect time to inquire what the good news of Christ they heard in our Sunday celebrations might mean in their lives. Tuscan ideas prove to be more than just plants and containers. After all, a great many saints traveled the countryside stopping to visit with strangers and ask them what the Word of God meant to them. We too are missionaries, not only of our rich tradition, but also of the living Word of God.

A sower went out to sow. And as he sowed, some seed fell on the path, and birds came and ate it up. Some fell on rocky ground, where it had little soil. It sprang up at once because the soil was not deep, and when the sun rose it was scorched, and it withered for lack of roots. Some seed fell among thorns, and the thorns grew up and choked it. But some seed fell on rich soil, and produced fruit, a hundred or sixty or thirtyfold. Whoever has ears ought to hear. MATTHEW 13:3-9

NOVEMBER

Pumpkin Seeds

A visitor to our parish from the Midwest (probably from those classic farmlands of our country) once looked at the vines growing on the grounds of Saint John Vianney and asked, "Are those vines I see pumpkins or wild gourds?"

I was tempted to fabricate a story with historical embellishments about the Native American Indians that inhabited our area. This temptation raced though my mind but I knew I would be busted! They are not wild gourds like the ones planted by Native Americans who once roamed the area. Those vines are the product of the seeds from giant pumpkins often placed in front of the altar for late autumn decor, the Interfaith Service, and of course, the liturgy on Thanksgiving Day. Since the first Sunday of Advent often falls on the Sunday after the Thursday of Thanksgiving, those giant orange vegetables find themselves rushed outside to sit on the south patio. That is, if no one adopts them for a pumpkin pie first. They have been known to sit outside right up until Christmas (and one year even until Valentine's Day!) After all, a few white lights and they become a novel Christmas decoration.

Once in a while, a concerned and caring parishioner (who shall remain nameless except for the moniker "General," or is it "Admiral" now? I forget her rank) is said to roll them over the parking lot to the bushes and gullies that surround the grounds. There they become food for the javelinas, deer, and our other wild residents. This course of action also results in broken pumpkin parts and spilled seeds everywhere. The seeds are blown, washed, or carried off. If the seed has any luck and finds sufficient moisture and soil it might try to root. These unlucky seeds attempt to germinate. Never has the condition been such that another pumpkin of equal size comes forth. In a lucky year maybe a small orange flower. More routinely the vines are eaten or they dry out before they have the opportunity to ramble around the rocky grounds.

Thankfully, we can be grateful that we don't dry out. If we but open our hearts and minds to God's love, we too can allow the soil of our hearts to be adequate grounds. The word of God will then bear fruit.

Scented Air

So be imitators of God, as beloved children, and live in love, as
Christ loved us and handed himself over for us as a sacrificial
offering to God for a fragrant aroma. EPHESIANS 5:1-2

There was the faint fragrance of a familiar essence. It triggered vague memories and a momentary mental abstraction, the remembrance of a much stronger aroma from years past. The priests coming for the Advent Reconciliation Service were forty-five minutes away. This was not quite enough time to become engrossed in any major endeavor. But the church itself was all ready for Advent with the birch trees and their blue lights in place. So there was a window of opportunity that allowed for a walk around the garden. A beautiful and unseasonably warm afternoon greeted any who were blessed to be out on this Monday following the first Sunday of Advent. This brief time of waiting provided the surprise of an opportunity to search for the origin of this fragrance. There it was. Of course—narcissus. Blooming on the

slopes between the asphalt parking lot and the quiet interior of the church were the clumps of straight narrow leaves and clusters of tiny white flowers. Alone on the banks among dormant deciduous trees and sleeping evergreens, flowers were about the only evidence of new life. They came from bulbs that had once graced the altar for the season of Advent years back and from the offspring of those original bulbs.

Only four days prior, the entire nation had attempted to slow down to celebrate Thanksgiving. It seemed the country had quickly rebounded. Advent, the season for preparation, calls for a slowing down in spite of a culture that speeds up with societal demands for an excessive Christmas. This late afternoon meander was in keeping with the spirit of Advent. It was indeed right in line with the Advent call to stop. It was an opportunity to ponder how great a blessing the Incarnation was and continues to be for us. It was a chance to be grateful for incredible blessings such as this very afternoon, that are continually showered on us. It was a time to slow down and enjoy life — a rare event for most of us.

Amazing! A mere bulb and its product of tiny white flowers perfumed the air for those who were coming to leave behind their burdens and begin again: . . . a woman came up to him with an alabaster jar of costly perfumed oil and poured it on his head while he was reclining at table. (Matthew 26:7). This man of course we know was Jesus. It is the same Christ who still comes to lift our burdens and give those who follow Him an opportunity to start over. A little bulb — hmmm. . .

And I tell you, ask and you will receive, seek and you will find; knock and the door will be opened to you. For everyone who asks, receives; and the one who seeks, finds; and to the one who knocks, the door will be opened. LUKE 11:9-10

DECEMBER

Cut, Living, or Artificial

Time has a tendency to distort our memories. It softens them, nuances them, often gives them a fondness that wasn't there originally. One constant in our lives, however, is that God's love is abundant! Our liturgical celebration should reflect this. Certain seasons not only call for "full, active, conscientious participation" (our mantra here at Saint John Vianney) but also for "conscious and conspicuous excess." This aspect of liturgy focuses our senses on the "over-the-top" love of our Creator. The Christmas season is just such a time.

Years ago, the idealistic-romantic "Peter Pan" tendencies of a younger pastor led him to think this could be accomplished by using as a backdrop evergreens bedecked with hundreds, maybe thousands, of tiny white lights. The youth group, along with some kind, idealistic-romantic "Wendy" type parishioners, indulged the priest. Off they trekked north to the Babbit family ranch to harvest, at the very least, thirty to fifty native piñons of all sizes and shapes to accomplish the task.

However, after this outing had been repeated annually for several years (the last one in bitter cold and snow), some questions arose. The remarks from concerned environmentalists, the maturing of the youth group participants, the aging of the "Wendys," as well as the presence of a stern fire chief, all nuanced the thinking of "Fr. Pan." A change was needed.

And so a new idea came to mind. Living trees would be incorporated into the art and environment of the church. These trees would be planted on the grounds after the Christmas celebrations. Different species, different types, different sizes could surround the altar (along with a

few cut trees snuck in at the back—no one will know!). This became the tradition for a few years. Those three-foot living trees that survived the hot lights and heated church are now planted on the grounds and have grown to over six times their original size. One is about eighteen feet tall. The blue spruces are absolutely beautiful when it snows. Actually, they all are gorgeous.

To stand next to one of those trees and look up at its tip brings a different question. How on earth could one person have carried in each hand a pot containing one of these living trees? From those initial snowy outings to living trees planted in mid-January have come living testimonies to how beautiful the sanctuary is each December. And more than that, a testimony to how beautiful our grounds continue to become.

Thus a progression of memories—from snowy outings and cut trees, to many parishioners taking countless trips to nurseries around northern Arizona to buy living ones, to slews of elves assembling artificial trees and hanging them with lights. It is a lesson: If we ask, a way is provided. Nuanced, of course—but nevertheless, oh, what a fond fond fond memory of how people throughout the ages have asked and it has been given. But then are not the nuances of life the very element that softens our memories? Are not the helping hands throughout the ages the element by which we have achieved our goals and desires?

Gifts

Consider this: whoever sows sparingly will also reap sparingly, and whoever sows bountifully will also reap bountifully. Each must do as already determined, without sadness or compulsion, for God loves a cheerful giver. Moreover, God is able to make every grace abundant for you, so that in all things, always having all you need, you may have an abundance for every good work.

2 CORINTHIANS 9:6-8

Christmas is fundamentally about God's gift to us. The gift of His Son—one like us. A gifted Son who grows, learns, experiences, and yet lives out the will of God no matter the obstacle. Therefore, we give gifts to one another in honor of the example of "giving" that we have been taught. It would be appropriate then to give something of one's self. Something that has been cared for, grown throughout the year. Well then, it should be most appropriate to take

some labor of love, the fruits of the garden, and incorporate them into gifts of the heart.

In summer, herbs are cut and hung from the kitchen ceiling to dry. These include chive blossoms, chilies, nopales, sprigs of rosemary, raisins from the grapevines, tiny lemons from the potted citrus trees, blackberries and raspberries from Oak Creek Canyon. Some of these come from plants that themselves were gifts from members of our family of faith. A gift becomes a gift becomes a gift. Juniper berries, piñon nuts, walnuts, almonds, and anything else the imagination recalls are gathered. Interesting bottles have been collected. They are purchased when found at the grocery, the drugstore, or the farmer's markets here and there. The botanicals collected over the year are coerced into the glassware. Then this glass bottle accumulation is topped off with olive oil, vinegar, or vodka to settle. It will set for the two or three months leading to the Christmas celebrations.

The garden is the result of many hands, of a multitude of giving hearts, and an abundance of love from so many over the years. Offshoots of plants, the cuttings, the extra sprouts, the stems, branches, bulbs, and the seeds of most everything found on the grounds of Saint John Vianney have been collected. It feels to me that our garden resembles one very tiny version of the Eden, or what I imagine Eden would be. It is most apropos, then, that the cycle of giving continues. Much like the continuing cycle of nature where plants sprout, grow, produce fruit, and begin over.

The gifts of our garden continue to give and be given in one unending cycle of love. Similar to the cycle of unconditional love the Creator has given us to share. We receive this love. It is nurtured and grows. When it is ripe it is shared with others. These gifts are but small moments of beauty that reflect the great moment of love when God gave His most precious gift.

ℰTHE ℰND.

Or rather the beginning (once again!)

This is how you are to pray:

Our Father in heaven, hallowed be your name, your kingdom come,

your will be done, on earth as in heaven. Give us today our daily

bread; and forgive us our debts, as we forgive our debtors; and do

not subject us to the final test, but deliver us from the evil one.

If you forgive others their transgressions, your heavenly Father

will forgive you. But if you do not forgive others, neither will your

Father forgive your transgressions. MATTHEW 6:9-15

Some of these writings sprang from hints contained in homilies, pastor's notes, and letters to the community from over the years. Most of the remembrances were triggered as I walked the grounds and the secret garden. I wonder what was forgotten or left out.

When I took the moments to ponder what should be included in "the Garden Book," so much came to mind — a flood of recollections from the last dozen years. That abundant flow is like what happens if I take the moments to thank God for extreme happiness and joy, and other moments to ask for guidance in times of confusion and frustration. I become so much more aware of my blessings.

Looking at the variety of green growing things in the garden of Saint John Vianney always brings people to mind. Some are named in these pages, but most are left in the special places of memory. It is the people of this family of faith that are represented by all the growing things. It is the people with their tender love that keep the promise of what can be.

The gardens of Saint John Vianney will never be complete, for that is the very nature of gardens — and of life itself. Nothing will ever be finished until that time when Jesus comes again in all His glory.

Until then, I hope that both family and strangers alike will find whatever they look for as they take time to be in God's presence while poking along the sidewalks and trails of the garden. In the garden we encounter and face authentically the drama of existence, the drama that includes the emotional and electrifying narrative of birth, the many and varied milestones of life, the poignant deaths, but, most importantly, the strength and power of our love for one for another. In the garden we encounter beauty and mystery. Most especially, we find there the ever-present unconditional love of God. This is the gift of the gardens of Saint John Vianney.

A Year in the Gardens of Saint John Vianney

Plants have many names, botanical and alternate botanical, family, genus and species names. There are common names, traditional, and regional names. There are names specific to particular neighborhoods. The following list contains the names I grew up associating with these plants. I ask your indulgence for any discrepancies. As this book illustrates, there are always "surprises" in gardening. I am not a master gardener, only a field hand in the vineyard.

January

18-19: Bell tower enhanced by honey locust branches (*Gleditsia triacanthos*)

20: Looking east from the shrine of St. Joseph and the Holy Child

22: Birch branch ice castle (*Betula nigra*)

23: The church in snow

25: Hybrid tea rose (*Rosa hybrids*), also 29

February

30: Dill blossom (*Anethum graveolens*)

31: Bearded white iris (*Iris germanica* 'tall bearded')

33: Begonia (*Begonia tuberosa*), rosemary (*Rosmarinus officinalis* 'Tuscan Blue'), lavender and other herbs and flowers

in the "secret garden"

35: St. Fiacre, patron saint of gardens

36: One of many angels that live in and protect the garden

37: Garlic chives (*Allium tuberosum*) under a Japanese maple (*Acer palmatum*)

39: Herb garden in oak barrels

41: West entrance of the church seen from the south driveway with Merry Go Round Rock in the background

42: Bernadette at Our Lady of Lourdes Shrine

45: Station of the Cross with spring flowers

March

46: Boston ivy (*Parthenocissus tricuspidata*) on the church wall

47: Young pine cones in spring

49: Potted cyclamen (*Cyclamen persicum*)

50: Jonaah waking up from a nap

51: Beloved (?) push mower

53: Bulbs waiting to be planted: King Alfred daffodils (*Narcissus* 'Trumpet') in the large basket, Dutch irises (*Iris reticulata*) in the small basket, ornamental onions (*Allium giganteum*) at far right

55: Miniature jonquil (*Narcissus jonquilla*)

April

56: Hybrid tea roses (*Rosa hybrids*), also 59, 63

57: Red ground cover shrub rose (*Rosa species*), also 62

58: Yellow rose (*Rosa hybrids*)

60: Shrine to Nuestra Señora de Guadalupe looking north toward the Wilson Mountain range

61: Shrine of Our Lady of Lourdes surrounded with red climbing roses (*Rosa species*)

64: Wisteria leaf (*Wisteria sinensis*)

67: Father and Child, the Shrine to St. Joseph

68-69: Golden coreopsis (*Coreopsis grandiflora*)

May

71: Oriental hybrid lilies (*Lilium oriental*), usually mixed with Easter Lilies (*Lilium longiflorum*) for Resurrection celebrations

73: Past year's lily resurrected again (*Lilium candidum*)

74: The 7th Station of the Cross, Jesus Falls the Second Time. Frémont cottonwood volunteer (*Populus fremontii*) and manzanita (*Arctostaphylos pungens*) in the foreground

77: Broom snakeweed (*Gutierrezia sarothrae*) enjoying the monsoon

79: Parry's Agave (*Agave parryi*)

80: A future Grand Canyon!

81: Temporary waterfall from a scupper on a parapet of the church and cane cholla (*Opuntia spinosior*)

82-83: Looking north from sanctuary windows towards Wilson Mountain and Brins Ridge

June

84: Evening Primrose (*Coreopsis grandiflora*) against a dry-stacked red rock wall

85: California poppy (*Eschscholzia californica*)

87: The 2nd Station of the Cross, Jesus Takes Up His Cross, in the springtime when plants are beginning to bloom

88: Evening Primrose (*Oenothera speciosa*) mingling with golden coreopsis (*Coreopsis grandiflora*)

89: Of course! Every garden needs pink flamingoes to bring us back to earth. These two nest with four others in the vinca (*Vinca major*) under the

crepe myrtle tree (*Lagerstroemia indica*)

90-91: ink evening primrose (*Oenothera speciosa*)

93: Lantana blossoms close up (*Lantana camara*)

94: Moth resting on pyrancantha buds (*Pyracantha coccinea*)

95: Looking up into the red maple forest (*Acer rubrum*)

97: Sugarbush blossom (*Rhus ovata*)

A Bend in the Year

100-101: Looking toward the eastern horizon at the Sail Rock and Steamboat Rock formations with telegraph plant (*Heterptheca psammophilia*) in foreground

102: Our prickly pear (*Opuntia engelmannii*) ridge, looking toward the Sphinx formation

103: *Opuntia engelmannii* wears its red clown noses in late summer

105: St. Joseph's Shrine

July

106: Golden coreopsis (*Coreopsis grandiflora*)

107: Crepe myrtle tree (*Lagerstroemia indica*), also 110

109: Bird house nestled among blooming photinia (*Photinia fraseri*) and Lady Banks rose (*Rosa banksiae*)

111: Crepe myrtle tree *Lagerstromeia indica*), pyracantha, and rose of sharon (*Hibiscus syriacus*) with a John F. Kennedy hybrid tea rose in front (*Rosa hybrid*)

113: A fountain on the west St. Francis ramada

114: Water lilies floating on the fish pond (*Nymphaeaceae nymphaea*)

115: Potted rosemary and garlic chives under a watchful angel

116-120: Water lilies (*Nymphaeaceae nymphaea*), goldfish and koi. Swimming things, buzzing things, blooming things. . .

August

122: The pondering chair on the Tuscany patio

123: Pathway through Fr.'s forest — pussy willow, river birch, red maples, Utah junipers, various pine trees, with vinca ground cover

125: A window to the imagination (*Pelargonium hortorum*)

126-127: Tomatoes! (*Lycopersicon esculentum*): a baby Big Boy, cherry tomatoes, romas, and a tomato flower

128-129: Peach trees (*Prunus persica*) like the high desert

130: Honey maker on pyrcantha blossoms (*Pyracantha coccinea*)

133: Engelmann's prickly pear *(Opuntia engelmannii)*

134: Potted succulents *(Crassulaceae echeveria)*, top, and Engelmann's prickly pear *(Opuntia engelmannii)*

135: *Opuntia engelmannii* and a view toward Sail Rock and Steamboat Rock

136: Agave *(Agave americana)*

137: Beavertail prickly pear *(Opuntia basilaris)* growing under manzanita *(Arctostaphylos pungens)*

138-139: *(Opuntia engelmannii)* dressed for winter, spring, summer, and fall

139: Cane cholla *(Opuntia spinosior)*

September

140: Seed packets and plant markers in preparation for fall planting

141: Quaking Aspen *(Populus tremuloides)* and cotoneaster *(Cotoneaster horizontalis)* with spiky red yucca *(Hesperaloe parviflora)* to the right

143: Pumpkin blossom *(Cucurbita maxima)* with a full pumpkin in background

144: Brown turkey fig tree *(Ficus carica)* with the potential of figs

145: Pointleaf manzanita *(Arctostaphylos pungens)* blossoms

147: Red Maple *(Acer rubrum)* against the crystal blue autumn sky

148: Wilson Mountain seen through the church's forest. Below: Vinca *(Vinca major)* at the bases of trees in "the forest"

149: "Mr. Stick," gently wrangled by Antonio Lopez for his photograph

150: Our signature cottonwood *(Populus fremontii)* whose roots are lifting the walkway (twelve years ago it was a three-inch sprout!)

152-153: Looking southwest from the north parking lot toward the east patio with the 7th Station, Jesus falls the second time, surrounded by older pines and younger trees

October

154: Agave *(Agave parry)*

155: Pyracantha berries *(Pyracantha coccinea)*

158-159: Red rock view with Coffeepot Rock, from the church grounds

161: Merlot grapes *(Vitis labrusca)* in the garden

162: An impromptu repast for drop-in guests with garden harvest quickly cut and wine (from the "cellar" under the bed)

November

165: Narcissus, also 170

167: Pumpkin blossom *(Cucurbita maxima)*

169: King Alfred daffodils *(Narcissus 'Trumpet')* waiting for their home in the soil

December

172: Snow on pine branches

173: One of the living Christmas trees *(Cedrus deodara)* provided by "The General"

175: Pine cones wait for Elementary Religious Education participants to transform them into treasures

176: A late afternoon winter snow on the west side of the church looking east to the Mund's Mountain Range, the Three Cross area dusted by snow

177: The East Patio in snow

178: Nuestra Señora de Guadalupe

180-181: Raffia-tied herbs drying in preparation for Christmas gifts

183: The gifts of the garden

185: Harvest moon above the Bell Tower

186: Hybrid tea rose *(Rosa hybrid)*

192: The gift of the garden

Thanks to our photographers: Al Brown: 2-3, 8, 10, 17, 18, 19, 20, 25, 30, 31, 39, 45, 47, 55, 57, 58, 59, 60, 61, 63, 68-69, 71, 74, 77, 78, 79, 80, 81, 82-83, 90-91, 93, 94, 97, 99, 106, 111, 113, 123, 126 bottom, 127 right, 130, 134 bottom, 136, 137, 138 left and center, 139 bottom, 140, 141, 145, 147, 148 bottom, 150, 152-153, 154, 155, 158-159, 165, 169, 170, 172, 173, 175, 180, 181, 183, 186, dustjacket back cover; **Michelle Dante:** 4, 27, 28, 33, 36, 38, 42, 64, 67, 95, 105, 114, 118, 119 top, 120, 121 top, 122, 125, 178,192, dustjacket spine; **David Halpern:** 1, dustjacket front cover; **J.C. Ortiz:** 23, 46, 49, 116, 117, 148 top, 176; **Dolores Puchi:** 22, 177; **Dave Singer:** 35, 37, 41, 50, 51, 53, 56, 62, 70, 73, 84, 85, 87, 88, 89, 93, 100-101, 102, 103, 107, 109, 110, 115, 119 bottom, 121 bottom, 126 top, 127 left, 128-129, 133, 134 top, 135, 138 right, 139 top, 143, 144, 161, 162, 164, 167, 185, inside front flap.